A MACDONALD BOOK
Text copyright © Margaret Linton and Trevor Terry 1989
Illustrations copyright © Tricia Newell 1989

First published in Great Britain in 1989
by Macdonald & Company (Publishers) Ltd
London & Sydney
A member of Maxwell Pergamon Publishing Corporation plc.

All rights reserved

Printed and bound in Great Britain by
Purnell Book Production Ltd
A member of BPCC plc

Main text set in 16pt Bembo Educational by Goodfellow & Egan Ltd

Macdonald & Co (Publishers) Ltd
66-73 Shoe Lane
London EC4P 4AB

British Library Cataloguing in Publication Data
Linton, Margaret, 1927–
   Squirrel is hungry.
   1. Squirrel – For children
   I. Title II. Terry, Trevor III. Series
   599.32′32

   ISBN 0–356–13890–9
   ISBN 0–356–13891–7 Pbk

• NATURE TALES •

SQUIRREL IS HUNGRY

Written by Margaret Linton and Trevor Terry
Illustrated by Tricia Newell

Macdonald

Grey Squirrel lived high up in an oak tree at the edge of the park.

His nest was made of twigs and leaves, and inside, it was lined with moss, dried grass and feathers. It kept Grey Squirrel safe and warm and dry.

One day Grey Squirrel woke up feeling very hungry.

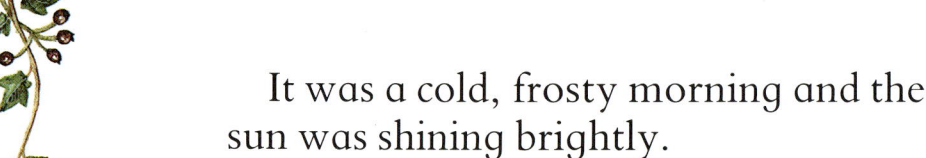

It was a cold, frosty morning and the sun was shining brightly.

Grey Squirrel sat up and looked around. He could see the park, the lake and some houses and gardens.

"I'm glad the sun is shining to-day," he thought. "I must look for some food. Perhaps I can find the acorns I buried in the Autumn."

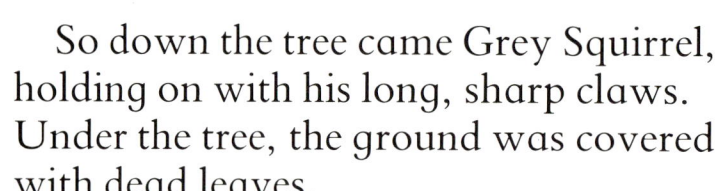

So down the tree came Grey Squirrel, holding on with his long, sharp claws. Under the tree, the ground was covered with dead leaves.

Grey Squirrel hopped about in the leaves, with his nose close to the ground. He sniffled and snuffled, and then began to dig. Soon he had found an acorn.

Grey Squirrel sat up and held the acorn in his paws. He didn't want to eat the outside of the acorn. That was too tough. So, using his sharp teeth, he peeled off the hard skin and nibbled the acorn until it was finished.

"That tasted good," he said to himself, "but I'm still hungry."

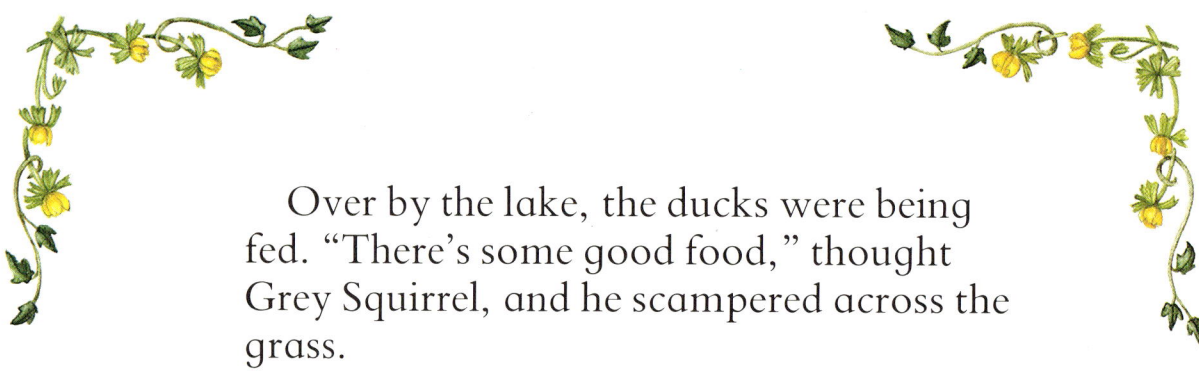

Over by the lake, the ducks were being fed. "There's some good food," thought Grey Squirrel, and he scampered across the grass.

Suddenly, a dog jumped out from behind a bush. Grey Squirrel ran up a tall pine tree, as fast as he could go.

"I'm glad dogs can't climb trees," he thought, "but I'm still hungry."

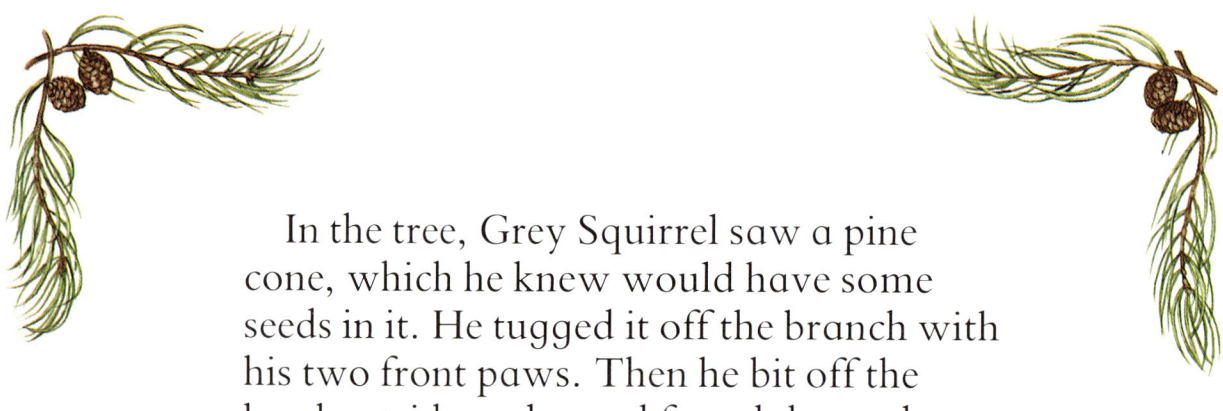

In the tree, Grey Squirrel saw a pine cone, which he knew would have some seeds in it. He tugged it off the branch with his two front paws. Then he bit off the hard outside scales and found the seeds inside.

"They tasted good," he said to himself, "but I'm still hungry."

Near the pine tree there was a house and garden. In the garden Grey Squirrel saw a bird table. There were lots of birds pecking at the food.

"M'm," thought Grey Squirrel. "I'll have some of that," and he ran down the trunk, climbed over a fence, and scampered over to the bird table.

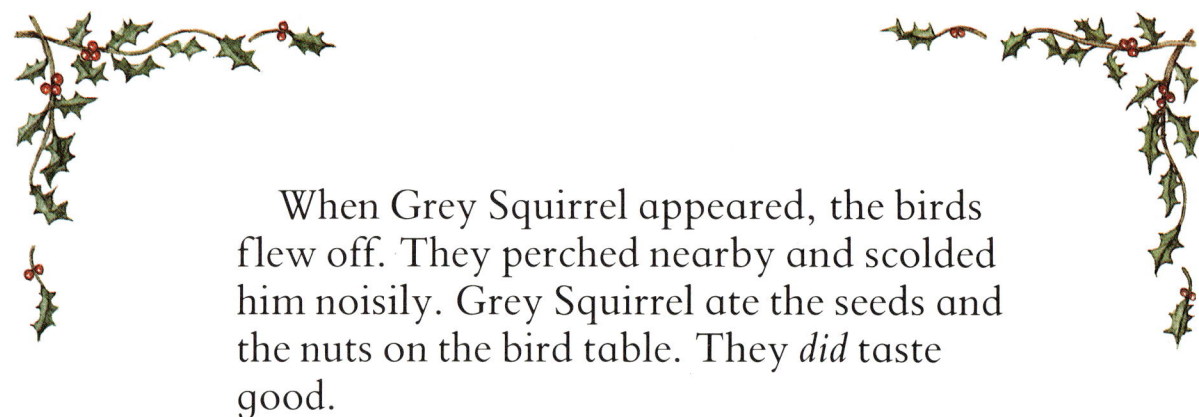

When Grey Squirrel appeared, the birds flew off. They perched nearby and scolded him noisily. Grey Squirrel ate the seeds and the nuts on the bird table. They *did* taste good.

Just then, a cat who had been watching the birds, sprang out and chased him away. He dashed up a tree and the cat climbed after him.

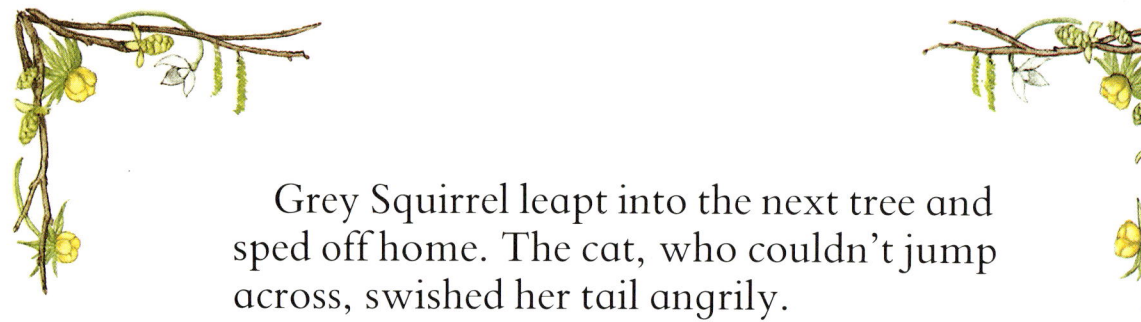

Grey Squirrel leapt into the next tree and sped off home. The cat, who couldn't jump across, swished her tail angrily.

"This has been my lucky day," thought Grey Squirrel. "I found food under the oak tree, in the pine tree and on the bird table. I'm not hungry now, but I do feel tired."

And he curled up in his nest and went to sleep.

holly berries

snowdrops

robin

cones

acorns

ivy